This planner belongs to

ISBN: 1483860906

SCHOOL _____

GRADE _____ ROOM _____

ADDRESS

_____

_____

_____

PHONE _____

DESIGNING MY OWN LIFE

LIKE A BOSS

MAKE YOUR MARK

CLASSROOM RESOURCES

IMPORTANT PASSWORDS

Professional Development

TITLE	DATE	HOURS

FAVORITE WEBSITES

Name

Contact Info

Schedule

SCHOOL BEGINS: _____

LUNCH: _____ RECESS: _____

SPECIALS: _____

_____

SCHOOL ENDS: _____

Need Help?

RELIABLE STUDENTS: _____

TEACHERS: _____

PRINCIPAL: _____

VICE PRINCIPAL: _____

OTHER STAFF: _____

Special Schedules

NAME	TIME/LOCATION
_____	_____
_____	_____
_____	_____
_____	_____

Additional Notes

_____

_____

_____

_____

_____

Communication Log

DATE	TYPE	NAME	PURPOSE	NOTES
	📱@☰👥			
	📱@☰👥			
	📱@☰👥			
	📱@☰👥			
	📱@☰👥			
	📱@☰👥			
	📱@☰👥			
	📱@☰👥			
	📱@☰👥			
	📱@☰👥			
	📱@☰👥			
	📱@☰👥			
	📱@☰👥			
	📱@☰👥			
	📱@☰👥			
	📱@☰👥			
	📱@☰👥			
	📱@☰👥			
	📱@☰👥			
	📱@☰👥			
	📱@☰👥			
	📱@☰👥			
	📱@☰👥			
	📱@☰👥			
	📱@☰👥			
	📱@☰👥			
	📱@☰👥			
	📱@☰👥			
	📱@☰👥			
	📱@☰👥			

Communication Log

DATE	TYPE	NAME	PURPOSE	NOTES
	📱@☰👫			
	📱@☰👫			
	📱@☰👫			
	📱@☰👫			
	📱@☰👫			
	📱@☰👫			
	📱@☰👫			
	📱@☰👫			
	📱@☰👫			
	📱@☰👫			
	📱@☰👫			
	📱@☰👫			
	📱@☰👫			
	📱@☰👫			
	📱@☰👫			
	📱@☰👫			
	📱@☰👫			
	📱@☰👫			
	📱@☰👫			
	📱@☰👫			
	📱@☰👫			
	📱@☰👫			
	📱@☰👫			
	📱@☰👫			
	📱@☰👫			
	📱@☰👫			
	📱@☰👫			
	📱@☰👫			
	📱@☰👫			

NOTES AND TO-DO'S

NOTES AND TO-DO'S

Plan It

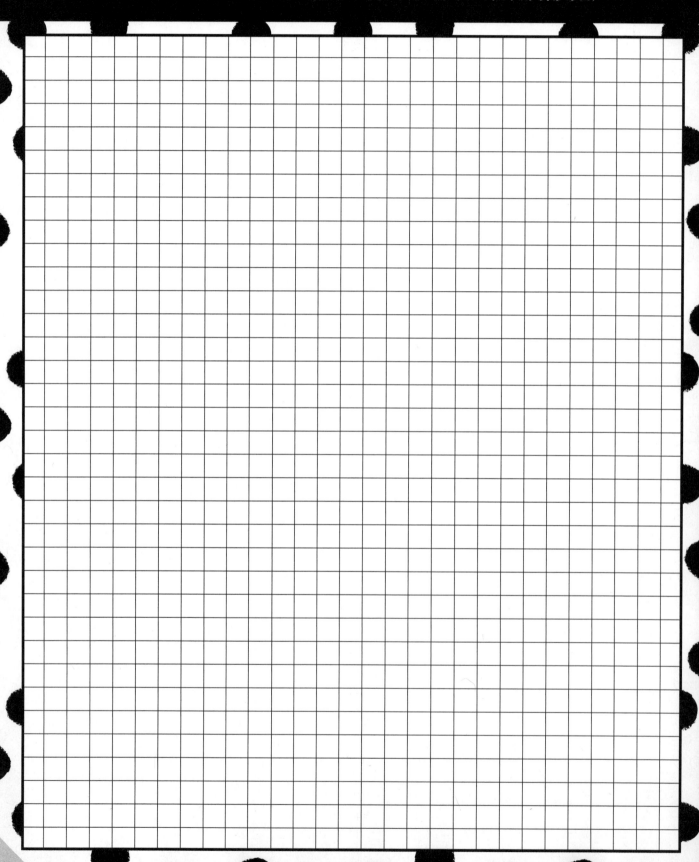

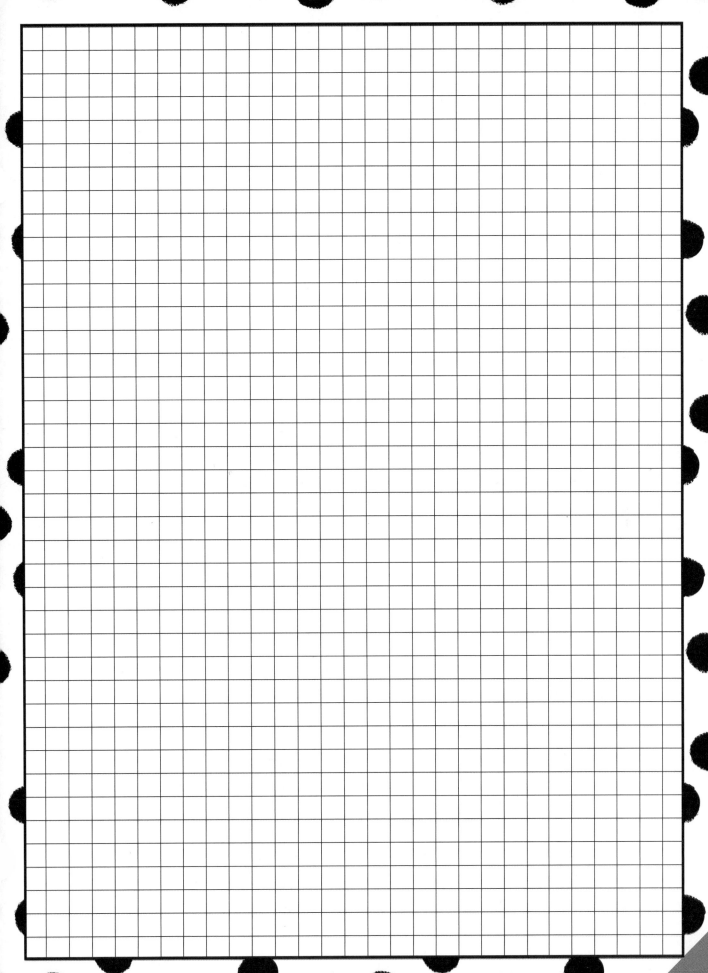

Year AT A *Glance*

JULY

AUGUST

SEPTEMBER

OCTOBER

NOVEMBER

DECEMBER

Year at a Glance

JANUARY

FEBRUARY

MARCH

APRIL

MAY

JUNE

JULY

Only the brave teach.

SUNDAY	MONDAY	TUESDAY	WEDNESDAY
○	○	○	○
○	○	○	○
○	○	○	○
○	○	○	○
○	○	○	○

THURSDAY	FRIDAY	SATURDAY	HAVE TO DO
◯	◯	◯	
◯	◯	◯	
◯	◯	◯	NOTES
◯	◯	◯	
◯	◯	◯	

Psst! Use these guides to keep your tabs perfectly placed.

AUGUST

Strive for progress, not perfection.

SUNDAY	MONDAY	TUESDAY	WEDNESDAY
○	○	○	○
○	○	○	○
○	○	○	○
○	○	○	○
○	○	○	○

THURSDAY	FRIDAY	SATURDAY	HAVE TO DO
○	○	○	
○	○	○	
○	○	○	NOTES
○	○	○	
○	○	○	

SEPTEMBER

Teaching is a work of heart.

SUNDAY	MONDAY	TUESDAY	WEDNESDAY
◯	◯	◯	◯
◯	◯	◯	◯
◯	◯	◯	◯
◯	◯	◯	◯
◯	◯	◯	◯

THURSDAY	FRIDAY	SATURDAY	HAVE TO DO
○	○	○	
○	○	○	
○	○	○	**NOTES**
○	○	○	
○	○	○	

OCTOBER

To teach is to touch a life forever.

SUNDAY	MONDAY	TUESDAY	WEDNESDAY
○	○	○	○
○	○	○	○
○	○	○	○
○	○	○	○
○	○	○	○

GOALS

THURSDAY	FRIDAY	SATURDAY	HAVE TO DO
○	○	○	
○	○	○	
○	○	○	NOTES
○	○	○	
○	○	○	

NOVEMBER

You are capable of amazing things.

SUNDAY	MONDAY	TUESDAY	WEDNESDAY
○	○	○	○
○	○	○	○
○	○	○	○
○	○	○	○
○	○	○	○

THURSDAY	FRIDAY	SATURDAY	HAVE TO DO
			NOTES

DECEMBER

See good in all things.

SUNDAY	MONDAY	TUESDAY	WEDNESDAY
◯	◯	◯	◯
◯	◯	◯	◯
◯	◯	◯	◯
◯	◯	◯	◯
◯	◯	◯	◯

GOALS

THURSDAY	FRIDAY	SATURDAY	HAVE TO DO
○	○	○	● _____
			● _____
			● _____
			● _____
○	○	○	● _____
			● _____
			● _____
			● _____
			● _____
			● _____
○	○	○	NOTES
			_____
			_____
			_____
○	○	○	_____
			_____
			_____
			_____
○	○	○	_____
			_____
			_____

JANUARY

Be your own kind of beautiful.

SUNDAY	MONDAY	TUESDAY	WEDNESDAY
◯	◯	◯	◯
◯	◯	◯	◯
◯	◯	◯	◯
◯	◯	◯	◯
◯	◯	◯	◯

THURSDAY	FRIDAY	SATURDAY	HAVE TO DO
◯	◯	◯	
◯	◯	◯	
◯	◯	◯	NOTES
◯	◯	◯	
◯	◯	◯	

FEBRUARY

Be the reason someone smiles today.

SUNDAY	MONDAY	TUESDAY	WEDNESDAY
○	○	○	○
○	○	○	○
○	○	○	○
○	○	○	○
○	○	○	○

THURSDAY	FRIDAY	SATURDAY	HAVE TO DO

NOTES

MARCH

Say yes to adventures.

SUNDAY	MONDAY	TUESDAY	WEDNESDAY
○	○	○	○
○	○	○	○
○	○	○	○
○	○	○	○
○	○	○	○

THURSDAY	FRIDAY	SATURDAY	HAVE TO DO
○	○	○	
○	○	○	
○	○	○	NOTES
○	○	○	
○	○	○	

APRIL

Wake up and be awesome.

SUNDAY	MONDAY	TUESDAY	WEDNESDAY
○	○	○	○
○	○	○	○
○	○	○	○
○	○	○	○
○	○	○	○

IMPORTANT DATES

GOALS

THURSDAY	FRIDAY	SATURDAY	HAVE TO DO
◯	◯	◯	
◯	◯	◯	
◯	◯	◯	NOTES
◯	◯	◯	
◯	◯	◯	

33

MAY

You are making a difference every day.

SUNDAY	MONDAY	TUESDAY	WEDNESDAY
○	○	○	○
○	○	○	○
○	○	○	○
○	○	○	○
○	○	○	○

THURSDAY	FRIDAY	SATURDAY	HAVE TO DO
○	○	○	
○	○	○	
○	○	○	**NOTES**
○	○	○	
○	○	○	

JUNE

It takes a big heart to shape little minds.

SUNDAY	MONDAY	TUESDAY	WEDNESDAY
○	○	○	○
○	○	○	○
○	○	○	○
○	○	○	○
○	○	○	○

IMPORTANT DATES

GOALS

THURSDAY	FRIDAY	SATURDAY	HAVE TO DO
○	○	○	
○	○	○	
○	○	○	NOTES
○	○	○	
○	○	○	

Week

	SUBJECT	SUBJECT	SUBJECT
MON. /			
TUE. /			
WED. /			
THUR. /			
FRI. /			

SUBJECT	SUBJECT	SUBJECT	SUBJECT

Psst! Cut this corner off each week to mark and find your place easily.

Week #		

	SUBJECT	SUBJECT	SUBJECT
MON. /			
TUE. /			
WED. /			
THUR. /			
FRI. /			

SUBJECT	SUBJECT	SUBJECT	SUBJECT

Week

MON.
/

TUE.
/

WED.
/

THUR.
/

FRI.
/

SUBJECT	SUBJECT	SUBJECT

SUBJECT	SUBJECT	SUBJECT	SUBJECT

		SUBJECT	SUBJECT	SUBJECT

Week

MON.
/

TUE.
/

WED.
/

THUR.
/

FRI.
/

SUBJECT	SUBJECT	SUBJECT	SUBJECT

Week #

MON.
/

TUE.
/

WED.
/

THUR.
/

FRI.
/

SUBJECT	SUBJECT	SUBJECT

SUBJECT	SUBJECT	SUBJECT	SUBJECT

Week

	SUBJECT	SUBJECT	SUBJECT
MON. /			
TUE. /			
WED. /			
THUR. /			
FRI. /			

SUBJECT	SUBJECT	SUBJECT	SUBJECT

Week
#

	SUBJECT	SUBJECT	SUBJECT
MON. /			
TUE. /			
WED. /			
THUR. /			
FRI. /			

SUBJECT	SUBJECT	SUBJECT	SUBJECT

SUBJECT	SUBJECT	SUBJECT	SUBJECT

SUBJECT	SUBJECT	SUBJECT	SUBJECT

SUBJECT	SUBJECT	SUBJECT	SUBJECT

SUBJECT	SUBJECT	SUBJECT

Week

	SUBJECT	SUBJECT	SUBJECT
MON. /			
TUE. /			
WED. /			
THUR. /			
FRI. /			

SUBJECT	SUBJECT	SUBJECT	SUBJECT

Week

	SUBJECT	SUBJECT	SUBJECT
MON. /			
TUE. /			
WED. /			
THUR. /			
FRI. /			

54

SUBJECT	SUBJECT	SUBJECT	SUBJECT

Week

	SUBJECT	SUBJECT	SUBJECT
MON. /			
TUE. /			
WED. /			
THUR. /			
FRI. /			

SUBJECT	SUBJECT	SUBJECT	SUBJECT

SUBJECT	SUBJECT	SUBJECT	SUBJECT

Week #		SUBJECT	SUBJECT	SUBJECT
MON. /				
TUE. /				
WED. /				
THUR. /				
FRI. /				

SUBJECT	SUBJECT	SUBJECT	SUBJECT

Week
#

MON.
/

TUE.
/

WED.
/

THUR.
/

FRI.
/

SUBJECT	SUBJECT	SUBJECT

SUBJECT	SUBJECT	SUBJECT	SUBJECT

Week

	SUBJECT	SUBJECT	SUBJECT
MON. /			
TUE. /			
WED. /			
THUR. /			
FRI. /			

SUBJECT	SUBJECT	SUBJECT	SUBJECT

SUBJECT	SUBJECT	SUBJECT	SUBJECT

SUBJECT	SUBJECT	SUBJECT	SUBJECT

SUBJECT	SUBJECT	SUBJECT	SUBJECT

SUBJECT	SUBJECT	SUBJECT	SUBJECT

Week #

	SUBJECT	SUBJECT	SUBJECT
MON. /			
TUE. /			
WED. /			
THUR. /			
FRI. /			

SUBJECT	SUBJECT	SUBJECT	SUBJECT

SUBJECT	SUBJECT	SUBJECT	SUBJECT

Week

MON. /

TUE. /

WED. /

THUR. /

FRI. /

SUBJECT	SUBJECT	SUBJECT

SUBJECT	SUBJECT	SUBJECT	SUBJECT

Week

	SUBJECT	SUBJECT	SUBJECT
MON. /			
TUE. /			
WED. /			
THUR. /			
FRI. /			

SUBJECT	SUBJECT	SUBJECT	SUBJECT

Week #

MON. /

TUE. /

WED. /

THUR. /

FRI. /

SUBJECT	SUBJECT	SUBJECT

SUBJECT	SUBJECT	SUBJECT	SUBJECT

Week

MON.
/

TUE.
/

WED.
/

THUR.
/

FRI.
/

SUBJECT	SUBJECT	SUBJECT

SUBJECT	SUBJECT	SUBJECT	SUBJECT

Week

SUBJECT	SUBJECT	SUBJECT

MON. /

TUE. /

WED. /

THUR. /

FRI. /

74

SUBJECT	SUBJECT	SUBJECT	SUBJECT

Week

	SUBJECT	SUBJECT	SUBJECT
MON. /			
TUE. /			
WED. /			
THUR. /			
FRI. /			

SUBJECT	SUBJECT	SUBJECT	SUBJECT

Week #

MON.
/

TUE.
/

WED.
/

THUR.
/

FRI.
/

SUBJECT	SUBJECT	SUBJECT

SUBJECT	SUBJECT	SUBJECT	SUBJECT

Week

	SUBJECT	SUBJECT	SUBJECT
MON. /			
TUE. /			
WED. /			
THUR. /			
FRI. /			

SUBJECT	SUBJECT	SUBJECT	SUBJECT

SUBJECT	SUBJECT	SUBJECT	SUBJECT

Week

\#

MON.

/

TUE.

/

WED.

/

THUR.

/

FRI.

/

SUBJECT	SUBJECT	SUBJECT

SUBJECT	SUBJECT	SUBJECT	SUBJECT

Week

	SUBJECT	SUBJECT	SUBJECT
MON. /			
TUE. /			
WED. /			
THUR. /			
FRI. /			

SUBJECT	SUBJECT	SUBJECT	SUBJECT

Week	SUBJECT	SUBJECT	SUBJECT
#			
MON. /			
TUE. /			
WED. /			
THUR. /			
FRI. /			

SUBJECT	SUBJECT	SUBJECT	SUBJECT

SUBJECT	SUBJECT	SUBJECT	SUBJECT

Week #

	SUBJECT	SUBJECT	SUBJECT
MON. /			
TUE. /			
WED. /			
THUR. /			
FRI. /			

SUBJECT	SUBJECT	SUBJECT	SUBJECT

Week

	SUBJECT	SUBJECT	SUBJECT
MON. /			
TUE. /			
WED. /			
THUR. /			
FRI. /			

SUBJECT	SUBJECT	SUBJECT	SUBJECT

Week

	SUBJECT	SUBJECT	SUBJECT
MON. /			
TUE. /			
WED. /			
THUR. /			
FRI. /			

SUBJECT	SUBJECT	SUBJECT	SUBJECT

SUBJECT	SUBJECT	SUBJECT	SUBJECT

SUBJECT	SUBJECT	SUBJECT	SUBJECT

SUBJECT	SUBJECT	SUBJECT	SUBJECT

SUBJECT	SUBJECT	SUBJECT	SUBJECT

Week

	SUBJECT	SUBJECT	SUBJECT
MON. /			
TUE. /			
WED. /			
THUR. /			
FRI. /			

94

SUBJECT	SUBJECT	SUBJECT	SUBJECT

Week #		SUBJECT	SUBJECT	SUBJECT
MON. /				
TUE. /				
WED. /				
THUR. /				
FRI. /				

SUBJECT	SUBJECT	SUBJECT	SUBJECT

SUBJECT	SUBJECT	SUBJECT	SUBJECT

SUBJECT	SUBJECT	SUBJECT	SUBJECT

SUBJECT	SUBJECT	SUBJECT	SUBJECT

SUBJECT	SUBJECT	SUBJECT	SUBJECT

Week

	SUBJECT	SUBJECT	SUBJECT
MON. /			
TUE. /			
WED. /			
THUR. /			
FRI. /			

SUBJECT	SUBJECT	SUBJECT	SUBJECT

Week
#

MON.
/

TUE.
/

WED.
/

THUR.
/

FRI.
/

SUBJECT	SUBJECT	SUBJECT

SUBJECT	SUBJECT	SUBJECT	SUBJECT

Week #

	SUBJECT	SUBJECT	SUBJECT
MON. /			
TUE. /			
WED. /			
THUR. /			
FRI. /			

SUBJECT	SUBJECT	SUBJECT	SUBJECT

Week #	SUBJECT	SUBJECT	SUBJECT
MON. /			
TUE. /			
WED. /			
THUR. /			
FRI. /			

SUBJECT	SUBJECT	SUBJECT	SUBJECT

SUBJECT	SUBJECT	SUBJECT	SUBJECT

Week #

	SUBJECT	SUBJECT	SUBJECT
MON. /			
TUE. /			
WED. /			
THUR. /			
FRI. /			

SUBJECT	SUBJECT	SUBJECT	SUBJECT

Week

	SUBJECT	SUBJECT	SUBJECT
MON. /			
TUE. /			
WED. /			
THUR. /			
FRI. /			

SUBJECT	SUBJECT	SUBJECT	SUBJECT

Week

#

	SUBJECT	SUBJECT	SUBJECT
MON. /			
TUE. /			
WED. /			
THUR. /			
FRI. /			

SUBJECT	SUBJECT	SUBJECT	SUBJECT

SUBJECT	SUBJECT	SUBJECT	SUBJECT

SUBJECT	SUBJECT	SUBJECT	SUBJECT

SUBJECT	SUBJECT	SUBJECT	SUBJECT

SUBJECT	SUBJECT	SUBJECT	SUBJECT

Week

	SUBJECT	SUBJECT	SUBJECT
MON. /			
TUE. /			
WED. /			
THUR. /			
FRI. /			

SUBJECT	SUBJECT	SUBJECT	SUBJECT

Week #		SUBJECT	SUBJECT	SUBJECT
MON. /				
TUE. /				
WED. /				
THUR. /				
FRI. /				

SUBJECT	SUBJECT	SUBJECT	SUBJECT

Week

	SUBJECT	SUBJECT	SUBJECT
MON. /			
TUE. /			
WED. /			
THUR. /			
FRI. /			

SUBJECT	SUBJECT	SUBJECT	SUBJECT

Student
CHECKLIST

name

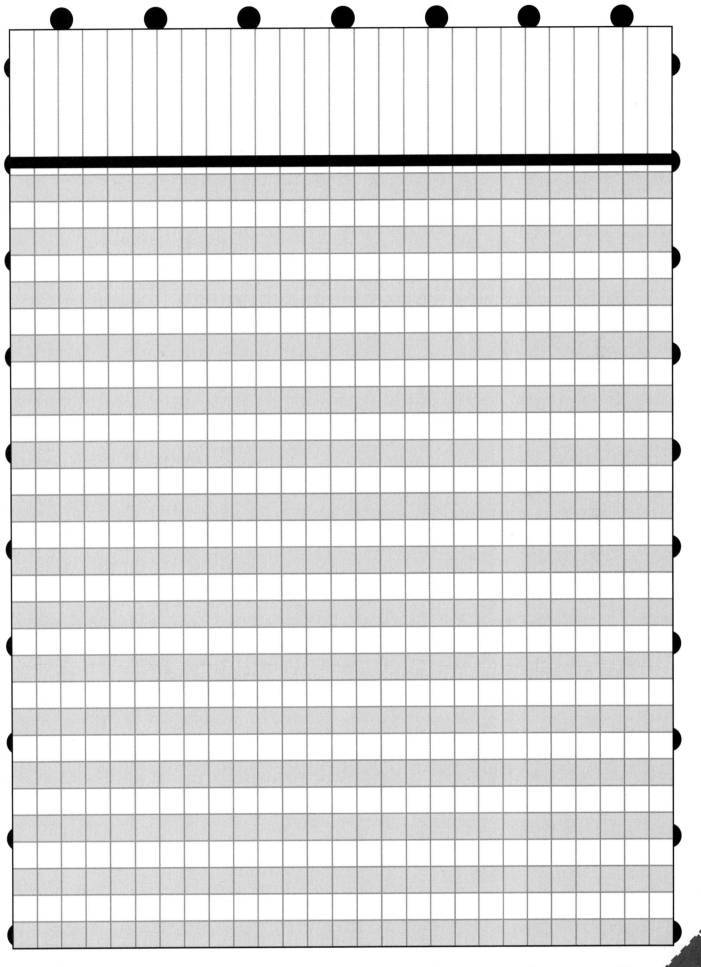

Student
CHECKLIST

name

FOLD OR CUT ALONG THIS LINE

120

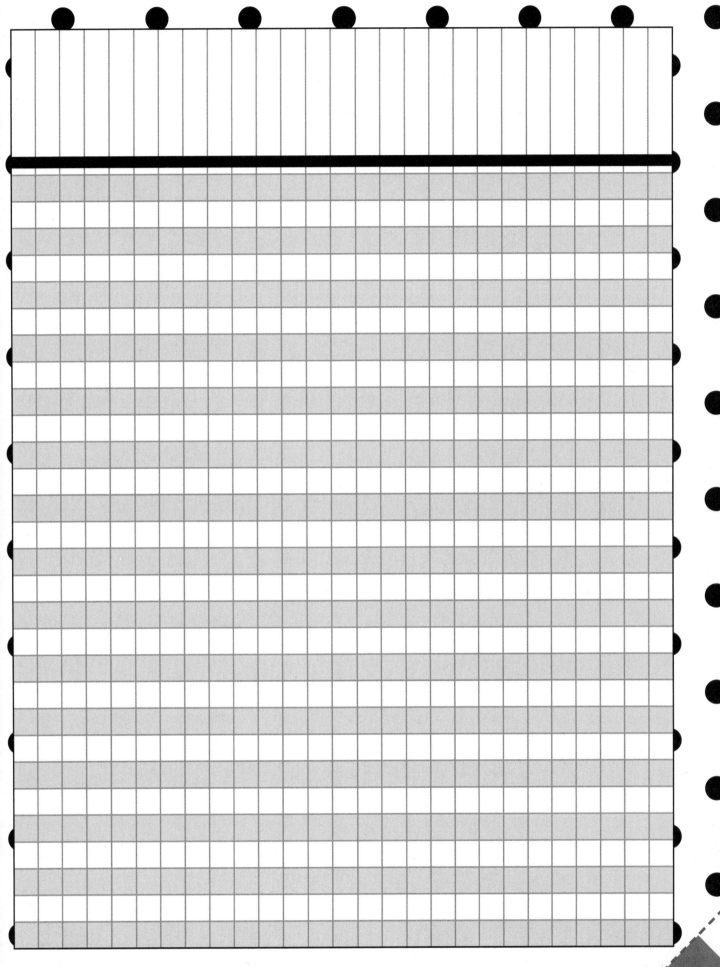

Student
CHECKLIST

name

FOLD OR CUT ALONG THIS LINE

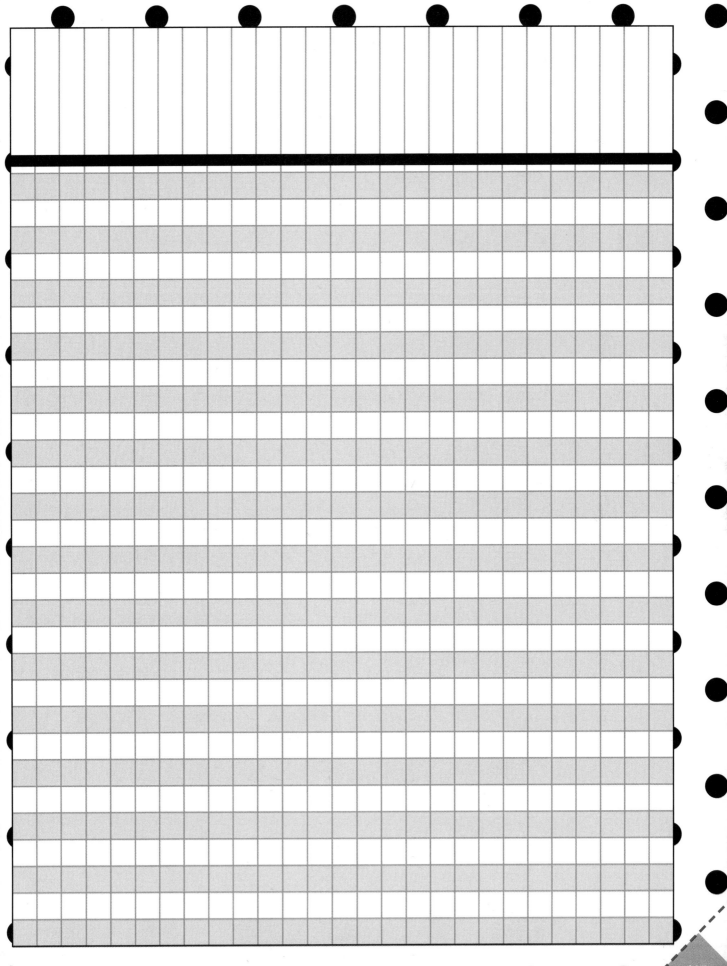

Student
CHECKLIST

name

FOLD OR CUT ALONG THIS LINE

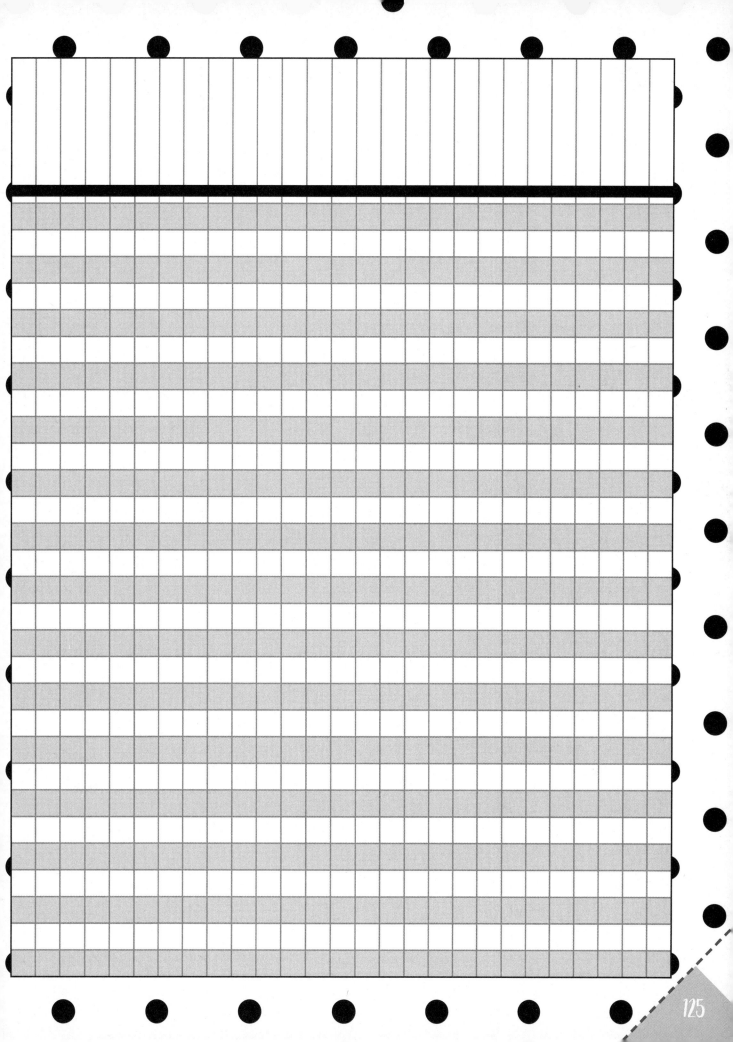

Student
CHECKLIST

name

FOLD OR CUT ALONG THIS LINE

126

WHEN GIVEN

the choice

BETWEEN BEING

right or being kind,

CHOOSE KIND.

—DR. WAYNE W. DYER